Crochet Potholders and Dishcloths

by Rita Weiss

Leisure Arts, Inc.
Maumelle, Arkansas

Produced by

Production Team

Creative Directors:	Jean Leinhauser and Rita Weiss
Technical Editors:	Mary Ann Frits and Kathy Wesley
Pattern Testers:	Susan Jeffers and Kim Britt
Book Design:	Linda Causee

Diagrams © 2015 by The Creative Partners™ LLC

Reproduced by special permission.

We have made every effort to ensure that these instructions are accurate and complete. We cannot, however, be responsible for human error, typographical mistakes or variations in individual work.

Published by Leisure Arts, Inc.

© 2015 by Leisure Arts, Inc.

104 Champs Boulevard, STE. 100

Maumelle, AR 72113-6738

www. leisurearts.com

ISBN-13: 978-1-4647-3371-0

Contents

Introduction

Looking to crochet a gift for someone who has just moved into a new house... something quick and easy, but something that will not only look beautiful but will be useful as well?

Or maybe you're looking for that very thing for yourself?

You've come to the right place, because in this book you'll find the answer you've been searching for.

Why not crochet a potholder or a dishcloth, two items that will not only be in constant use, but will add a bit of delightful décor to any kitchen.

A dishcloth need not only be used for cleaning but can add some fun décor to your kitchen. A potholder shaped like a football player or a wise owl can serve not only to hold a hot pot but can also make a great accent piece in your kitchen.

A dishcloth is ready for use as soon as you put down your crochet hook, but potholders often require additional work to prepare them for their job. There are many different ways to do this; basically a potholder requires crocheting two pieces and joining the two pieces together. Crocheting only one piece and then backing your potholder with cotton fabric intended for a quilt is another option. The important thing to remember about the materials used to crochet a potholder is to always use cotton thread. Polyester thread could not only allow heat to pass through to your hands, but it could cause your completed potholder to melt as you hold an especially hot pot.

As you crochet your dishcloth and your potholder, remember that these beautifully crocheted pieces serve more than utilitarian purposes. They also add to the décor in your kitchen as they liven up your counter tops, your walls and your towel racks with clever and attractive accent pieces.

So get out your crochet hooks and your crochet thread, and join us for a fun adventure creating something wonderful.

Pretty Panda Oven Mitt

Designed by Susan Lowman

Let our Pet Panda help you create a fantastic dinner to amaze your family and friends as you take the food from the oven.

SKILL LEVEL

Intermediate

FINISHED SIZE

Approx 6" wide x 10¼" high (15.24 cm x 26.03 cm)

MATERIALS

Size 3 crochet thread

[100% mercerized cotton, 150 yards (137.16 meters) per ball]

    2 balls white

    2 balls black

    Small amount green

Note: *Photographed model made with Aunt Lydia's® Crochet Thread Fashion 3™ #201 White, #12 Black and #625 Sage.*

Size G/6 (4 mm) crochet hook (or size required for gauge)

Size D/3 (3.25 mm) crochet hook (or size required for gauge)

2 black safety eyes, 12 mm diameter

1 black safety nose, 20 mm wide

Stitch marker

Tapestry needle

GAUGE

With larger hook and 2 strands of thread, 18 sc = 4" (10.16 cm)

STITCH GUIDE

Single crochet decrease (sc dec): (Insert hook in next st and draw up a lp) twice, YO and draw through all 3 lps on hook: sc dec made.

INSTRUCTIONS

Note: *To change colors, work last st of old color until 2 lps rem on hook, drop old color and pick up new color, YO with new color and draw through 2 lps on hook.*

Front (use larger hook and 2 strands of thread throughout)

Row 1 (right side): Starting at bottom of body and working up to top of head with white, ch 22, sc in back bump of 2nd ch from hook and in back bump of each rem ch across: 21 sc; ch 1, turn.

Row 2: Work 2 sc in first sc, sc in each sc across to last sc, 2 sc in last sc: 23 sc; ch 1, turn.

Row 3: Repeat Row 2: 25 sc.

Rows 4 through 20: Sc in each sc across; ch 1, turn. At end of Row 20, change to black in last sc.

Row 21: With black, sc in each sc across; ch 1, turn.

Row 22: Sc dec in first 2 sc, sc in each sc across to last 2 sc, sc dec in last 2 sc: 23 sc; ch 1, turn.

Row 23: Sc in each sc across; ch 1, turn.

Row 24: Repeat Row 22: 21 sc.

Row 25: With black, sc in first 6 sc, changing to white in last sc; with white, sc in next 9 sc, changing to black in last sc; with black, sc in last 6 sc; ch 1, turn.

Row 26: With black, sc dec in first 2 sc, sc in next 2 sc, changing to white in last sc; with white, sc in next 13 sc, changing to black in last sc; with black, sc in next 2 sc, sc dec in last 2 sc: 19 sc; ch 1, turn.

Row 27: With black, sc in first sc, changing to white; with white, sc in next 17 sc, changing to black in last sc; with black, sc in last sc; ch 1, turn.

Row 28: With white, sc in each sc across; ch 1, turn.

Row 29: Work 2 sc in first sc, sc in each sc across to last sc, 2 sc in last sc: 21 sc; ch 1, turn.

Rows 30 through 33: Repeat Rows 28 and 29, twice: 23 sc in Row 31: 25 sc in Row 33.

Rows 34 through 38: Repeat Row 28, 5 times.

Rows 39 through 45: Sc dec in first 2 sc, sc in each sc across to last 2 sc, sc dec in last 2 sc: 2 less sc in each row than in previous row (23 sc in Row 39, 11 sc in Row 45); ch 1, turn. At end of Row 45, do not ch 1. Finish off; weave in ends.

Edging

With right side facing, work 1 round of sc evenly around edges of entire piece, matching row colors throughout; join with sl st in first sc. Finish off; weave in ends.

Back

Rows 1 through 17: Work same as Rows 1 through 17 on Front.

Row 18: Sc in first 5 sc, place stitch marker in last sc made, ch 15, skip next 15 sc (thumb opening made), sc in last 5 sc: 10 sc and 1 ch-15 sp; ch 1, turn.

Row 19: Sc in first 5 sc, sc in each of next 15 chs, sc in last 5 sc: 25 sc; ch 1, turn.

Rows 20 through 45: Work same as Rows 20 through 45 on Front.

Edging

Work same as edging on Front.

Thumb Piece

Row 1 (wrong side): With larger hook and 2 strands of white, join with sl st on wrong side of edge of marked sc on Row 18 of Back, with wrong side facing, sc in each skipped sc on Row 17 of thumb opening, sl st in edge of next sc on Row 18: 15 sc; ch 1, turn.

Note: *Work now proceeds in joined, turned rounds.*

Round 1 (right side): Skip sl st, sc in each sc on Row 1, skip sl st, sc in free loop of each of 15 chs of thumb opening; join with sl st in first sc: 30 sc; ch 1, turn.

Note: *First sc in Rounds 2 through 14 is worked in same sc as joining.*

Rounds 2 through 6: Sc in each sc around; join as before; ch 1, turn.

Round 7: (Sc dec in next 2 sc, sc in next 11 sc, sc dec in next 2 sc) twice; join: 26 sc; ch 1, turn.

Round 8: Repeat Round 2.

Round 9: (Sc dec in next 2 sc, sc in next 9 sc, sc dec in next 2 sc) twice; join: 22 sc; ch 1, turn.

Round 10: Repeat Round 2.

Round 11: (Sc dec in next 2 sc, sc in next 7 sc, sc dec in next 2 sc) twice; join: 18 sc; ch 1, turn.

Round 12: Repeat Round 2.

Round 13: (Sc dec in next 2 sc, sc in next 5 sc, sc dec in next 2 sc) twice; join: 14 sc; ch 1, turn.

Round 14: Sc in each sc around; join. Finish off, leaving a long tail for sewing. Fold Thumb Piece in half and whip stitch 7 stitches on each half together. Weave in ends.

Ears (make 2)

Row 1 (wrong side): Starting at bottom with larger hook and 2 strands of black, ch 3, sc in 2nd ch from hook, 2 sc in next ch; working in free lp(s) on opposite side of chs, 2 sc in first ch, sc in next ch: 6 sc; ch 1, turn.

Row 2 (right side): Sc in first sc, 2 sc in each of next 4 sc, sc in last sc: 10 sc; ch 1, turn.

Row 3: Sc in first 3 sc, 2 sc in next sc, sc in next 2 sc, 2 sc in next sc, sc in last 3 sc: 12 sc; ch 1, turn.

Edging

Work 2 sc in first sc, sc in next 2 sc, (2 sc in next sc, sc in next sc, 2 sc in next sc) twice, sc in next 2 sc, 3 sc in last sc; working across edge of rows, sc in edge of

Rows 2 and 1, sc in beg ch, sc in edge of Rows 1 through 3; join with sl st in first sc: 25 sc. Finish off; weave in ends.

Eye Patches (make 2)

Row 1 (wrong side): Starting at top with larger hook and 2 strands of black, ch 3, sc in 2nd ch from hook and in next ch: 2 sc; ch 1, turn.

Row 2 (right side): Work 2 sc in first sc, sc in next sc: 3 sc; ch 1, turn.

Row 3: Sc in each sc across; ch 1, turn.

Row 4: Sc in first sc, sc dec in last 2 sc: 2 sc; ch 1, turn.

Row 5: Repeat Row 3.

Edging

Sc in first sc, 2 sc in next sc, sc in edge of next 4 rows, 2 sc in free lp of each beg ch, sc in edge of next 5 rows; join with sl st in first sc: 16 sc. Finish off, leaving a long tail for sewing.

Arms (make 2)

Row 1: Starting at bottom with larger hook and 2 strands of black, ch 10, sc in 2nd ch from hook and in each ch across: 9 sc; ch 1, turn.

Row 2: Work 2 sc in first sc, sc in next 7 sc, 2 sc in last sc: 11 sc; ch 1, turn.

Row 3: Sc in first 9 sc, sc dec in last 2 sc: 10 sc; ch 1, turn.

Row 4: Sc dec in first 2 sc, sc in last 8 sc: 9 sc; ch 1, turn.

Row 5: Work 2 sc in first sc, sc in next 2 sc, sc dec in next 2 sc: 5 sc; ch 1, turn, leaving rem sc unworked.

Row 6: Sc in each sc across; ch 1, turn.

Row 7: Sc dec in first 2 sc, sc in next 2 sc, 2 sc in last sc; ch 1, turn.

Row 8: Sc in first 3 sc, sc dec in last 2 sc: 4 sc; ch 1, turn.

Row 9: Sc dec in first 2 sc, sc in next sc, 2 sc in last sc; ch 1, turn.

Row 10: Repeat Row 6.

Row 11: Repeat Row 9.

Row 12: Sc dec in first 2 sc, sc dec in last 2 sc: 2 sc.

Edging

On one piece, ch 1, turn. On other piece, ch 1, but do not turn. Sc evenly around entire piece; join. Finish off, leaving a long tail for sewing.

Feet (make 2)

Round 1 (right side): With larger hook and 2 strands of black, ch 2, 6 sc in 2nd ch from hook; join with sl st in first sc: 6 sc.

Round 2: Work 2 sc in same sc as joining and in each sc around; join as before: 12 sc.

Round 3: Sc in same sc as joining, 2 sc in next sc, (sc in next sc, 2 sc in next sc) 5 times; join: 18 sc.

Round 4: Work 2 sc in same sc as joining, sc in next 2 sc, 2 sc in next sc, hdc in next 2 sc, 3 dc in next sc, dc in next 2 sc, 3 dc in next sc, hdc in next 2 sc, (2 sc in next sc, sc in next 2 sc) twice; join: 26 sts. Finish off, leaving a long tail for sewing.

Branch

With smaller hook and 1 strand of green, ch 22; *sl st in 2nd ch from hook, hdc in next 2 chs, sl st in next 2 chs (leaf made)*; ch 9, repeat from * to * to make 2nd leaf; ch 8, repeat from * to * to make 3rd leaf; sl st in next 2 chs, sl st in ch at base of 2nd leaf, sl st in next 2 chs, ch 6, repeat from * to * to make 4th leaf; sl st in ch at base of 4th leaf, sl st in next ch, sl st in ch at base of first leaf, sl st in next 2 chs, ch 6, repeat from * to * to make 5th leaf; sl st in ch at base of 5th leaf, sl st in each rem ch of beg ch-22: 5 leaves. Finish off, leaving a long tail for sewing.

Assembly

Weave in all ends that were not left long for sewing. Attach safety eyes through middle of Row 2 of Eye Patches, then through 8th st from each edge of Row 37 of Front. Angle Eye Patches as shown in photograph on page 4 and sew edges of Eye Patches to Front, using a running stitch through edging of Eye Patches. Attach safety nose in middle of Row 32 of Front. With 2 strands of black and tapestry needle, sew mouth below nose, as shown in photograph,

or as desired. Arrange Branch on Front, as shown in photograph,
and sew Branch down. Sew Arms and Feet to Front, using a running stitch through edging of Arms and through last round of Feet, overlapping one Arm over Branch, as shown in photograph. With wrong sides of Front and Back together and using 2 strands of white, sew head of Front and Back together, inserting Ears in place between Front and Back (with right side of Ears facing Front) and sewing through bottom edge of Ears at same time, using running stitch through edging of Front and Back. Using 2 strands of matching color, sew left and right edges of black section that is below head together on Front and Back, then sew left and right edges of body together on Front and Back, using running stitch through edging of Front and Back. Leave bottom edge of Front and Back open to insert hand.

Finishing

If desired, line inside of oven mitt with fabric.

Fabulous Fish Potholder

If you're planning a fish dinner, be sure to add this Fancy Fish to your guest list.

SKILL LEVEL

Intermediate

FINISHED SIZE

Approx 6½" wide by 8½" long (16.51 cm x 21.59 cm) including fins and tail

MATERIALS

Size 10 crochet thread [0]

[100% mercerized cotton, 350 yds (320 meters) per ball]

> 2 balls dark blue
>
> 1 ball medium blue
>
> 1 ball red

Note: *Photographed model made with Aunt Lydia's® Crochet Thread Classic 10™ #487 Dark Royal, #480 Delft and #494 Victory Red.*

Steel Crochet Hook No. 4 (2 mm) (or size required for gauge)

Blunt-end sewing needle

GAUGE

7 sc = 1" (2.54 cm) with two strands of thread

INSTRUCTIONS

Note: *Double strand of thread is used throughout.*

Front

With a double strand of dark blue, ch 53.

Row 1: Sc in 2nd ch from hook and in each rem ch: 52 sc. Turn.

Row 2 (right side): Finish off one strand of dark blue, join one strand of medium blue. Sl st in first 2 sc, sc in next 4 sc, hdc in next 4 sc, dc in next 6 sc, tr in next 20 sc, dc in next 6 sc, hdc in next 4 sc, sc in next 4 sc, sl st in last 2 sc. Break off medium blue. Turn.

Row 3: Join second strand of dark blue. Sl st in first 2 sl sts, sc in each st across to last 2 sl sts, sl st in last 2 sl sts. Turn.

Rows 4 through 7: Repeat Rows 2 and 3 twice more.

Row 8: Repeat Row 2.

Finish off.

With wrong side facing and beg ch at top, attach a double strand of dark blue in first unused lp of beg ch, sc in each rem lp: 52 sc. Turn.

Repeat Rows 2 through 8. Fasten off.

Edging

With right side facing, join a double strand of dark blue in the first sl st of final Row 8. Sc in same st and in each st across to last sl st on row.

Work clusters across end sts as follows: ch 3, skip first end stitch and keeping last loop of each dc on hook, dc in end st of next 3 rows, yarn over and pull through all 4 lps on hook.

Repeat cluster over next 3 end sts, ch 3, (cluster over next 3 end sts) twice (this will be the face end); ch 3, sc in first sl st on opposite side, sc in each st across to last sl st at other end, (cluster over next 3 end sts) 4 times, ch 3, join with a sl st.

Finish off.

Referring to photo, and the face end, embroider eye and mouth with straight stitches, using two strands of red thread.

Back

Work same as for Front; do not embroider eye and mouth.

Fins (Make 3)

With double strand of dark blue, ch 2.

Round 1: 6 sc in 2nd ch from hook: 6 sc. Mark beg of round.

Round 2: 2 sc in each sc: 12 sc.

Round 3: * Sc in next sc, 2 sc in next sc; repeat from * 5 times more: 18 sc.

Round 4: * Sc in next 2 sc, 2 sc in next sc; repeat from * 5 times more: 24 sc.

Round 5: * Sc in next 3 sc, 2 sc in next sc; repeat from * 5 times more: 30 sc.

Round 6: * Sc in next 4 sc, 2 sc in next sc; repeat from * 5 times more: 36 sc.

Finish off.

Fold each Fin (circle) in half. With dark blue, sew sides together to create semi-circle.

Tailfins (Make 2)

Work same as for Fins.

Finishing

Edge Row: Holding front and back with wrong sides together, join a double strand of dark blue thread at one end and working through both thicknesses, sc completely around the potholder.

Referring to the photo, sew the Fins and Tailfins to the final edge row using dark blue thread and sewing needle. Finish off.

Hanger

With two strands of medium blue, insert hook into the ch-3 space between clusters at Face End. Ch 15; join in first sc to form a ring. Ch 1, 20 sc in ring. Join with sl st into first sc. Finish off.

Tomato Potholder

If you're planning to add tomatoes to your dinner, don't forget to add this potholder to hold your masterpiece.

SKILL LEVEL

Intermediate

FINISHED SIZE

Approx 10" (25.40 cm) diameter

MATERIALS

Size 10 crochet thread

[100% mercerized cotton, 350 yds (320 meters) per ball]

      2 balls red

      1 ball green

Note: *Photographed model made with Aunt Lydia's® Crochet Thread Classic 10™ #494 Victory Red and #397 Wasabi.*

Steel Crochet Hook No. 4 (2 mm) (or size required for gauge)

GAUGE

7 sc = 1" (2.54 cm) with two strands of thread

STITCH GUIDE

Picot: Ch 3, sl st in 3rd ch from hook: picot made.

INSTRUCTIONS

Note: *Double strand of thread is used throughout.*

Front

Row 1: Leaving a long tail, ch 5, sl st into 5th ch from hook to join and form a ring, ch 1, turn.

Row 2 (right side): (Work sc, hdc, dc, 3 tr, 5 dc, 3 tr, dc, hdc, sc) into ring, join with sl st into first sc: 17 sts; ch 1, turn.

Row 3: Sc in first sc, hdc in next st, dc in next st, 2 dc in next st, dc in next st, tr in next 3 sts, * dc in next 2 sts, 2 dc in next st; repeat from * 5 times more; tr in next 3 sts, dc in next st, 2 dc in next st, dc in next st, hdc in next st, sc in last sc, join: 41 sts; ch1, turn.

Row 4: Sc in first sc, * 2 sc in next st, sc in next 2 sts; repeat from * to last sc, sc in last sc, join: 54 sts; ch1, turn.

Row 5: Sc in first sc, * 2 dc in next st, dc in next 2 sts; repeat from * around to last sc, sc in last sc, join: 71 sts; ch 1, turn.

Row 6: Sc into first sc and in each st around, join; ch1, turn.

Row 7: Sc in first sc, hdc in next sc, * 2 dc in next sc, dc in next 3 sc; repeat from * around to last 2 sc, hdc in next sc, sc in last sc, join: 88 sts; ch 1, turn.

Row 8: Repeat Row 6.

Row 9: Sc in first sc, hdc in next sc, 2 dc in next sc, (dc in next sc, 2 dc in next sc) 3 times; * dc in next 4 sc, 2 dc in next sc; repeat from * to last 9 sc, (dc in next sc, 2 dc in next sc) 3 times; 2 dc in next sc, hdc in next sc, sc in last sc, join: 102 sts; ch 1, turn.

Row 10: Repeat Row 6.

Row 11: Sc in first sc, hdc in next sc, 2 dc in next sc, (dc in next sc, 2 dc in next sc) 3 times; * dc in next 5 sc, 2 dc in next sc; repeat from * to last 9 sc, (dc in next sc, 2 dc in next sc) 3 times; 2 dc in next sc, hdc in next sc, sc in last sc, join: 116 sts; ch 1, turn.

Row 12: Repeat Row 6.

Row 13: Sc in first sc, hdc in next sc, 2 dc in next sc, (dc in next sc, 2 dc in next sc) 3 times; * dc in next 5 sc, 2 dc in next sc; repeat from * to last 9 sc, (dc in next sc, 2 dc in next sc) 3 times; 2 dc in next sc, hdc in next sc, sc in last sc, join: 130 sts; ch 1, turn.

Row 14: Repeat Row 6.

Row 15: Sc in the back lp of each sc around; join with sl st in first sc.

Finish off.

Back

Make same as Front.

Leaf and Stem (Make 2)

With 4 strands of green, ch 6, dtr in 6th ch from hook, picot; ch 5, sc in same ch as dtr, (ch 5, dtr in same ch as last dtr, picot, ch 5, sc in same ch as last dtr) twice; ch 25, sc in 2nd ch from hook and in next 16 ch, sl st in side of first sc made on stem, sc in each rem ch, sl st in base of leaf. Break off.

Assembly

Place wrong sides of potholder together and whip stitch around. Referring to the photo, sew one set of leaves in place on front and one set of leaves in place on the back. Match the wrong sides of the stems together and whipstitch along their sides to complete the stem. Finish off and weave in ends.

Pretty Petals Potholder

Instead of a bouquet of flowers decorating your dining table, use this floral motif to decorate your potholder.

SKILL LEVEL

Easy

SIZE

Approx 8" (20.32 cm) in diameter

MATERIALS

Size 3 crochet thread

[100% mercerized cotton, 150 yards (137.16 meters) per ball]

    1 ball rose

Note: *Photographed model made with Aunt Lydia's® Crochet Thread Fashion 3™ #775 Warm Rose.*

Size E/4 (3.5 mm) crochet hook (or size required for gauge)

Wool felt to match

Cotton quilt batting

Sewing needle and thread

GAUGE

Rounds 1 to 3 = 2½" (6.35 cm) in diameter.

INSTRUCTIONS

Starting at center, ch 5, join with a sl st in first ch to form a ring.

Round 1: Ch 1, 15 sc in ring; join with a sl st in first sc: 15 sc.

Round 2: Ch 1, sc in same sc as joining, * ch 3, skip next 2 sc, sc in next sc, repeat from * around, skip beg ch-3; join with a sl st in first sc: 5 ch-3 lps.

Round 3: * (Sc, hdc, 3 dc, hdc, sc) in next ch-3 lp: petal made. Repeat from * around; join with a sl st in first sc.

Round 4: Ch 2, * holding next petal forward, sl st in base of center dc behind petal, ch 3, repeat from * around; skip beg ch-2, join with a sl st in first sl st.

Round 5: Repeat Round 3.

Round 6: Ch 1, * holding next petal forward, sl st in base of first hdc behind petal, ch 3, sl st in base of last hdc of same petal, ch 3, repeat from * around, skip beg ch-1, join with sl st in first sl st: 10 lps.

Round 7: Repeat Round 3: 10 petals.

Round 8: Ch 1, * holding next petal forward, sl st in base of first hdc, behind petal, ch 3, sl st in base of last hdc of same petal, ch 3, repeat from * around; skip beg ch-1, join with sl st in first sl st: 20 lps.

Round 9: Repeat Round 3: 20 petals.

Round 10: Ch 2, * holding next petal forward, sl st in base of center dc behind petal, ch 3, repeat from * around; skip beg ch-2, join with sl st in first sl st.

Round 11: (Sc, hdc, 3 dc, hdc, sc) in each ch-3 lp around; join with sl st in first sc: 20 petals.

Round 12: Ch 2, * holding next petal forward, sl st in base of center dc behind petal, ch 3, repeat from * around; skip beg ch-2, join with sl st in first sl st.

Round 13: (Sc, hdc, 3 dc, hdc, sc) in each ch-3 lp around; join with sl st in first sc: 20 petals.

Round 14: Ch 1, * (holding next petal forward, sl st in base of center dc of petal, ch 3) 3 times, holding next petal forward, sl st in base of first hdc behind petal, ch 3, sl st in base of last hdc of same petal, ch 3; repeat from * around, skip beg ch-1, join with a sl st in first sl st: 25 lps.

Round 15: Repeat Round 3: 25 petals.

Round 16: Ch 2, * holding next petal forward, sl st in base of center dc behind petal, ch 3, repeat from * around; skip beg ch-2, join with sl st in first sl st.

Round 17: (Sc, hdc, 3 dc, hdc, sc) in each ch-3 lp around; join with sl st in first sc .

Round 18: Ch 2, * holding next petal forward, sl st in base of center dc behind petal, ch 3, repeat from * around; skip beg ch-2, join with a sl st in first sl st.

Round 19: (Sc, hdc, 3 dc, hdc, sc) in each ch-3 lp around; join with sl st in first sc: 25 petals.

Round 20: Ch 2, * holding next petal forward, sl st in base of center dc behind petal, ch 4, repeat from * around; skip beg ch-2, join with a sl st in first sl st.

Round 21: (Sc, hdc, 5 dc, hdc, sc) in each ch-4 lp around; join with sl st in first sc: 25 petals.

Finish off.

Hanger

Join thread in space between any 2 petals on Round 21. Ch 15, join in first ch to form a ring. Ch 1, 20 sc in ring, join in first sc. Finish off. Weave in all ends.

Finishing

Cut 2 thicknesses of cotton quilt batting and 1 layer of felt to fit back of Potholder. Layer as follows: potholder with wrong side facing up, 2 layers of cotton quilt batting, felt backing on top. Whipstitch in place.

Note: *Use cotton quilt batting for center of potholder and wool felt for the lining. Polyester batting could allow heat to pass through to your hands, causing burns. If you wash the wool felt before using it to line the potholder, you'll take care of any additional shrinkage that may occur with laundering.*

Wonderful Watermelon Potholder

A potholder that mimics a watermelon is an attractive addition to your kitchen.

SKILL LEVEL

Easy

FINISHED SIZE

Approx 10" (25.4 cm) diameter

MATERIALS

Size 10 crochet thread

[100% mercerized cotton, 350 yds (320 meters) per ball]

    1 ball rose

    1 ball green

    1 ball white

Note: *Photographed model made with Aunt Lydia's® Crochet Thread Classic 10™ #493 French Rose, #484 Myrtle Green, #1 White*

Steel Crochet Hook No. 4 (2 mm) (or size required for gauge)

GAUGE

7 dc = 1" (2.54 cm) with two strands of thread

INSTRUCTIONS

Note: *Double strand of thread is used throughout.*

Top

Starting at center with 2 strands of rose, ch 4.

Round 1: 11 dc in 4th ch from hook. Join with sl st in 3rd ch of beg ch-4: 12 dc.

Round 2: Ch 3, dc in same ch as joining, 2 dc in each dc around. Join with sl st in 3rd ch of beg ch-3: 24 dc.

Round 3: Ch 3, dc in same ch as joining, * dc in next dc, 2 dc in next dc; repeat from * around. Join: 36 dc.

Round 4: Ch 3, dc in same ch as joining, * dc in next 2 dc, 2 dc in next dc; repeat from * around. Join: 48 dc.

Round 5: Ch 3, dc in same ch as joining, * dc in next 3 dc, 2 dc in next dc; repeat from * around. Join: 60 dc.

Round 6: Ch 3, dc in same ch as joining, * dc in next 4 dc, 2 dc in next dc; repeat from * around. Join: 72 dc.

Round 7: Ch 3, dc in same ch as joining, * dc in next 5 dc, 2 dc in next dc; repeat from * around. Join: 84 dc.

Round 8: Ch 3, dc in same ch as joining, * dc in next 6 dc, 2 dc in next dc; repeat from * around. Join: 96 dc.

Round 9: Ch 3, dc in same ch as joining, * dc in next 7 dc, 2 dc in next dc; repeat from * around. Join: 108 dc.

Round 10: Ch 3, dc in same ch as joining, * dc in next 8 dc, 2 dc in next dc; repeat from * around. Join: 120 dc.

Round 11: Ch 3, dc in same ch as joining, * dc in next 9 dc, 2 dc in next dc; repeat from * around, changing to white in last dc. Join: 132 dc. Finish off rose.

Round 12: Ch 3, dc in same ch as joining, * dc in next 10 dc, 2 dc in next dc; repeat from * around. Join: 144 dc.

Round 13: Ch 3, dc in same ch as joining, * dc in next 11 dc, 2 dc in next dc; repeat from * around, changing to green in last dc. Join: 156 dc. Finish off white.

Round14: Ch 3, dc in same ch as joining, * dc in next 12 dc, 2 dc in next dc; repeat from * around. Join: 168 dc.

Round 15: Ch 3, dc in same ch as joining, * dc in next 13 dc, 2 dc in next dc; repeat from * around. Join: 180 dc. Finish off green.

Bottom

Using two strands of Rose, repeat Rounds 1 through 13 of Potholder Top, changing to green in the last dc. Join and finish off Rose. Work Rounds 14 and 15 in green. Finish off.

Finishing

Place Top and Bottom together with wrong sides facing. Using 2 strands of green, crochet the two pieces together by working an sc evenly around. Fold the potholder in half; using the green, sew the ends together 1" along both sides.

Weave in all ends.

Hanger

Join 2 strands of green near fold at one end of potholder. Ch 15, join in first ch to form a ring. Work 20 sc in first ring. Finish off. Weave in all ends.

My Favorite Quarterback Potholder

Designed by Susan Lowman

Having a Super Bowl party? Crochet this potholder, that you'll use to take the food off the grill, in your team's colors.

SKILL LEVEL

Intermediate ▆▆▆▢

FINISHED SIZE

Approx 6½" wide x 10" high (16.51 cm x 25.40 cm)

MATERIALS

Size 3 crochet thread

[100% mercerized cotton, 150 yards (137.16 meters) per ball]

> 2 balls black
>
> 2 balls red
>
> 2 balls white
>
> 2 balls light brown
>
> 1 ball dark brown

Note: *Photographed model made with Aunt Lydia's® Crochet Thread Fashion 3™ #12 Black, #6 Scarlett, #201 White, 310 Copper Mist and #365 Coffee*

Size G/6 (4 mm) crochet hook (or size required for gauge)

¾" bone ring or plastic ring

Stitch marker

Tapestry needle

GAUGE

With larger hook and 2 strands of thread, 18 sc = 4" (10.16 cm)

STITCH GUIDE

Single crochet decrease (sc dec): (Insert hook in next st and draw up a lp) twice, YO and draw through all 3 lps on hook: sc dec made.

Extended single crochet (esc): Insert hook in specified st and draw up a lp, YO and draw through 1 lp on hook, YO and draw through both lps on hook: esc made.

Foundation single crochet (fsc):

First fsc: Insert hook in same st as last sc made and draw up a lp, YO and draw through 1 lp on hook (base ch made), YO and draw through both lps on hook: fsc made.

Additional fsc: Insert hook in 2 lps of base ch on last fsc made and draw up a lp, YO and draw through 1 lp on hook (base ch made), YO and draw through both lps on hook: fsc made.

Notes:

To change colors, work last st of old color until 2 lps rem on hook, drop old color and pick up new color, YO with new color and draw through 2 lps on hook.

To join with sc, make a slip knot and place on hook, insert hook in specified st and draw up a lp, YO and draw through both lps on hook.

To join with sc dec, make a slip knot and place on hook, insert hook in first specified st and draw up a lp, insert hook in 2nd specified st and draw up a lp, YO and draw through all 3 lps on hook.

Instructions

Note: *Double strand of thread is used throughout.*

Front (Use larger hook and 2 strands of thread.)

Row 1 (right side): Starting at bottom of body and working up to top of head, with black, ch 16, sc in back bump of 2nd ch from hook and in back bump of each rem ch across: 15 sc; ch 1, turn.

Row 2: Work 2 sc in first sc, sc in each sc across to last sc, 2 sc in last sc: 17 sc; ch 1, turn.

Row 3: Repeat Row 2: 19 sc.

Row 4: Repeat Row 2: 21 sc.

Row 5: Sc in each sc across; ch 1, turn.

Row 6: Repeat Row 2, changing to red in last sc: 23 sc.

Row 7: With red, sc in back lp of each sc across; ch 1, turn.

Row 8: Repeat Row 2: 25 sc.

Rows 9 and 10: Repeat Row 5 twice.

Row 11: Repeat Row 2: 27 sc.

Rows 12 through 23: Repeat Row 5 twelve times.

Row 24: Sc dec in first 2 sc, sc in each sc across to last 2 sc, sc dec in last 2 sc: 25 sc; ch 1, turn.

Row 25: Repeat Row 5.

Rows 26 and 27: Repeat Rows 24 and 25: 23 sc.

Row 28: Repeat Row 24: 21 sc.

Row 29: Sc in first 5 sc, changing to light brown in last sc; with light brown, sc in next 11 sc, changing to red in last sc; with red, sc in last 5 sc; ch 1, turn.

Row 30: Sc in first 3 sc, changing to light brown in last sc; with light brown, sc in next 15 sc, changing to red in last sc; with red, sc in last 3 sc, changing to light brown in last sc; ch 1, turn.

Rows 31 through 39: With light brown, repeat Row 5 nine times.

Row 40: Repeat Row 24: 19 sc.

Row 41: Repeat Row 5.

Rows 42 and 43: Repeat Rows 40 and 41: 17 sc.

Rows 44 through 48: Repeat Row 24 five times: 7 sc at end of Row 48. Do not ch 1 at end of Row 48. Finish off; weave in ends.

Edging

With right side facing, sc evenly around entire piece, increasing at curves as needed, matching colors throughout; join with sl st in first sc. Finish off; weave in ends.

Back
(use larger hook and 2 strands of thread throughout)

Rows 1 through 28: Work same as Rows 1 through 28 on Front.

Right-hand Edge

Row 29: Sc in first 4 sc, sl st in next sc: 4 sc; turn, leaving rem sts unworked.

Row 30: Skip sl st, sl st in next sc, sc in last 3 sc: 3 sc. Finish off; weave in ends.

Left-hand Edge

Row 29: With right side facing, skip next 11 unworked sc on Row 28, join red with sl st in next sc, sc in last 4 sc: 4 sc; ch 1, turn.

Row 30: Sc in first 3 sc, sl st in next sc. Finish off; weave in ends.

Back Helmet

Row 1 (right side): With right side facing, join white with sc in back lp of first sc on Row 30, sc in back lp of next 2 sc, sc in back lp of next sl st, skip Row 29, sc in back lp of same sc on Row 28 where sl st was worked on Row 29, sc in back lp of next 11 sc on Row 28, sc in back lp of same sc on Row 28 where sl st was worked on Row 29, skip Row 29, sc in back lp of sl st on Row 30, sc in back lp of next 3 sc: 21 sc; ch 1, turn.

Row 2: Sc in first 4 sc, esc in next 13 sc, sc in last 4 sc: 21 sts; ch 1, turn.

Row 3: Sc in first 3 sc, esc in next 15 sc, sc in last 3 sc; ch 1, turn.

Rows 4 through 9: Sc in each st across.

Rows 10 through 18: Repeat Rows 40 through 48 on Front. Finish off; weave in ends.

Edging

With right side facing, sc evenly around entire piece, increasing at curves as needed, matching colors throughout; join with sl st in first sc. Finish off; weave in ends.

Front Helmet
(use larger hook and 2 strands of thread throughout)

Row 1: Starting in middle of helmet and working toward top, with white, ch 20, sc in back bump of 2nd ch from hook and in back bump of each rem ch across: 19 sc; ch 1, turn.

Row 2: Sc dec in first 2 sc, sc in each sc across to last 2 sc, sc dec in last 2 sc: 17 sc; ch 1, turn.

Row 3: Sc in each sc across; ch 1, turn.

Rows 4 through 8: Repeat Row 2 five times: 7 sc at end of Row 8. Do not ch 1 at end of Row 8. Finish off; weave in ends.

First Ear Section

Row 1: With wrong side of Front Helmet facing and beg ch at top, working in free lps of beg ch with larger hook, join 2 strands of white with sc in first ch, sc in same ch, sc dec in next 2 sc: 3 sc; ch 1, turn, leaving rem chs unworked.

Rows 2 through 9: Sc in each sc across; ch 1, turn. At end of Row 9, do not ch 1. Finish off; weave in ends.

Second Ear Section

Row 1: With wrong side of Front Helmet facing and beg ch at top, working in free lps of beg ch with larger hook, sk next 13 unworked chs, join 2 strands of white with sc dec in next 2 sc, 2 sc in last sc: 3 sc; ch 1, turn.

Rows 2 through 9: Sc in each sc across; ch 1, turn. At end of Row 9, do not finish off.

Edging

Sc evenly around entire helmet, increasing and decreasing as needed; join with sl st in first sc. Finish off, leaving a long tail for sewing.

Face Mask

With smaller hook and 1 strand of black, ch 16; * sl st in back bump of 2nd ch from hook, sl st in back bump of next 7 chs *, ch 13; repeat from * to *; ch 15; repeat from * to *; ch 13; repeat from * to *; straighten out piece, remove hook from lp, insert hook in back bump of first ch made and pull lp through ch, sl st in back bump of next ch after last sl st made before removing hook (place marker in this st), sl st in back bump of each rem ch around center of piece; join with sl st in marked sl st. Finish off, leaving a long tail for sewing.

Helmet Stripes (Make 2)

With smaller hook and 1 strand of black, ch 45, sl st in back bump of 2nd ch from hook and in back bump of each rem ch across: 44 sl sts. Finish off, leaving a long tail for sewing.

Eyes (Make 2)

Rnd 1 (right side): With smaller hook and 1 strand of black, ch 2, 6 sc in 2nd ch from hook; join with sl st in first sc: 6 sc. Finish off, leaving a long tail for sewing.

First Arm (use larger hook and 2 strands of thread thoughout)

Row 1 (wrong side): Starting at top with red, ch 2, 3 sc in 2nd ch from hook: 3 sc; ch 1, turn.

Rows 2 and 3: Sc in each sc across; ch 1, turn. At end of Row 3, change to light brown in last sc.

Row 4: With light brown, sc in back lp of each sc across; ch 1, turn.

Row 5: Work 2 sc in first sc, sc dec in last 2 sc; ch 1, turn.

Rows 6 and 7: Sc in each sc across; ch 1, turn.

Row 8: Sc in each sc across, ch 7; turn.

Row 9: Sc in 2nd ch from hook and in next 5 chs, sc in next 3 sc: 9 sc; ch 1, turn.

Row 10: Sc in each sc across. Ch 1, do NOT turn.

Edging

Sc evenly around entire piece, increasing and decreasing as needed, matching colors; join with sl st in first sc. Finish off, leaving a long tail for sewing.

Second Arm (use larger hook and 2 strands of thread thoughout)

Rows 1 through 4: Work same as Rows 1 through 4 on First Arm.

Row 5: Sc dec in first 2 sc, 2 sc in last sc; ch 1, turn.

Rows 6 through 8: Sc in each sc across; ch 1, turn.

Row 9: Sc in each sc across, work 6 fsc: 9 sc; ch 1, turn.

Row 10: Sc in each st across. Ch 1, do NOT turn.

Edging

Sc evenly around entire piece, increasing and decreasing as needed, matching colors; join with sl st in first sc. Finish off, leaving a long tail for sewing.

Football

Row 1 (wrong side): With smaller hook and 1 strand of dark brown, ch 2, 2 sc in 2nd ch from hook: 2 sc; ch 1, turn.

Row 2 (right side): Work 2 sc in each sc: 4 sc; ch 1, turn.

Row 3: Work 2 sc in first sc, sc in next 2 sc, 2 sc in last sc: 6 sc; ch 1, turn.

Rows 4 through 6: Sc in each sc across; ch 1, turn.

Row 7: Sc dec in first 2 sc, sc in next 2 sc, sc dec in last 2 sc: 4 sc; ch 1, turn.

Row 8: Sc dec in first 2 sc, sc dec in last 2 sc: 2 sc; ch 1, turn.

Row 9: Sc dec: 1 sc; ch 1, turn.

Edging

Sc evenly around football, increasing at ends; join with sl st in first sc. Finish off, leaving a long tail for sewing.

Football Stripes

With right side facing, and 1 strand of white, sew stripes and lines on football, referring to photo for placement.

Hanging Loop

With smaller hook and 1 strand of black, join with sc around bone ring, work 23 more sc around ring: 24 sc; join with sl st in first sc. Finish off, leaving a long tail for sewing.

Assembly

With wrong side of Front and Back pieces together, sew around all edges, matching colors. Referring to photograph for placement, sew Face Mask to Front. Sew Front Helmet to Front, overlapping side edges of Face Mask. Sew Eyes to Front. Center Helmet Stripes on Front and Back Helmet and sew in place. Sew Arms to Front and Football between arms. Center covered bone ring at top of potholder and sew in place.

Corn on the Cob Pan Holder

Cooking a dish with corn? Clasp the pan handle with this pan holder.

SKILL LEVEL

Intermediate

FINISHED SIZE

Approx 2½" wide x 6¾" long (5.08 cm x 17.15 cm)

MATERIALS

Size 10 crochet thread

[100% mercerized cotton, 350 yards (320 meters) per ball]

      1 ball yellow

      1 ball green

Note: *Photographed model made with Aunt Lydia's®️ Crochet Thread Classic 10™️ #423 Maize and #449 Forest Green.*

Size 7 (4.5 mm) crochet hook (or size required for gauge)

1" diameter bone ring

Tapestry needle

GAUGE

32 sc = 4" (10.16 cm)

STITCH GUIDE

Popcorn (PC): Work 5 dc in specified st or sp, drop lp from hook, insert hook in first dc of 5 dc just made and draw dropped lp through tightly: PC made.

Single crochet decrease (sc dec): (Insert hook in next st and draw up a lp) twice, YO and draw through all 3 lps on hook: sc dec made.

INSTRUCTIONS

Corn (make 2)

Row 1 (right side): With yellow, ch 56, sc in 2nd ch from hook, sc in next ch, hdc in next ch, dc in next ch, [PC in next ch, dc in next ch] 24 times, hdc in next ch, sc in last 2 chs: 24 PC; ch 1, turn.

Row 2: Sc in each st across: 55 sc; ch 1, turn.

Row 3: Sc in first 2 sts, hdc in next st, dc in next st, (PC in next st, dc in next st) 24 times, hdc in next st, sc in last 2 sts: 24 PC; ch 1, turn.

Row 4: Sc in each st across: 55 sc; ch 1, turn.

Rows 5 through 16: Repeat Rows 3 and 4 six times. At end of Row 16, do not ch 1. Finish off; weave in ends.

Leaves (make 3)

Row 1 (right side): With green, ch 3, dc in 3rd ch from hook, ch 1, 8 sc around post of dc: 8 sc; ch 1, turn.

Rows 2 through 11: Sc in each sc across; ch 1, turn.

Row 12: Sc dec in first 2 sc, sc in each sc across to last 2 sc, sc dec in last 2 sc: 6 sc; ch 1, turn.

Rows 13 through 15: Repeat Row 2 three times.

Row 16: Repeat Row 12: 4 sc.

Row 17: Repeat Row 2.

Row 18: Sc dec in first 2 sc, sc dec in last 2 sc: 2 sc; ch 1, turn.

Row 19: Sc dec in 2 sc: 1 sc. Finish off, leaving a long tail for sewing.

Ring

With green, work 50 sc around bone ring; join with sl st in first sc. Finish off, leaving a long tail for sewing.

Assembly

With wrong sides of corn together, sew pieces together lengthwise at both long sides, leaving 1½" (3.8 cm) opening at one short end (or enough to fit desired pan handle). Close opening at other short end by gathering the edges together firmly. Sew covered ring to center of closed end of corn, as shown. Sew leaves to closed end of corn with 1 leaf on front and 2 leaves on back of corn.

Cucumber Pan Holder

What a great decorative addition to your cooking!

SKILL LEVEL

Intermediate

FINISHED SIZE

Approx 2⅝" wide x 6¾" long (6.67 cm x 17.15 cm)

MATERIALS

Size 10 crochet thread

[100% mercerized cotton, 350 yards (320 meters) per ball]

    1 ball green

Note: *Photographed model made with Aunt Lydia's® Crochet Thread Classic 10™ #449 Forest Green.*

Size 7 (4.5 mm) crochet hook (or size required for gauge)

1" diameter bone ring

Tapestry needle

GAUGE

38 sts in pattern = 4" (10.16 cm)

STITCH GUIDE

Single crochet decrease (sc dec): (Insert hook in next st and draw up a lp) twice, YO and draw through all 3 lps on hook: sc dec made.

INSTRUCTIONS

Cucumber (make 2)

Row 1 (right side): Ch 65, sc in 2nd ch from hook, sc in next 3 chs; * (sc, dc) in next ch, skip next ch; repeat from * 27 more times; sc in last 4 chs: 28 dc and 36 sc; ch 1, turn.

Row 2: Sc in first 4 sc; * skip next dc, (sc, dc) in next sc; repeat from * 27 more times; sc in last 4 sc; ch 1, turn.

Rows 3 through 19: Repeat Row 2, 17 times. At end of Row 19, do not ch 1. Finish off; weave in ends.

Tendrils (make 5)

Row 1 (right side): Make a chain 1½" (3.81 cm) long, sl st in 2nd ch from hook and in each rem ch. Finish off, leaving a long tail for sewing.

Ring

Work 50 sc around bone ring; join with sl st in first sc. Finish off, leaving a long tail for sewing.

Assembly

With wrong sides of cucumbers together, sew pieces together lengthwise at both long sides, leaving 1½" (3.8 cm) opening at one short end (or enough to fit desired pan handle). Close opening at other short end by gathering the edges together firmly. Sew covered ring to center of closed end of cucumber, as shown. Sew tendrils to closed end of cucumber, as shown.

Mr. Owl Potholder

Designed by Susan Lowman

If it's true that the owl is a wise bird, then surely you'll want Mr. Owl to help make the party a success.

Additional colorways
shown on front cover.

SKILL LEVEL

Easy ▐▬▭▭

FINISHED SIZE

Approx 6½" wide x 9½" high (16.5 cm x 24.13 cm)

MATERIALS

Size 3 crochet thread

[100% mercerized cotton, 150 yards (137.16 meters) per ball]

For each potholder: 2 balls of desired color (blue, pink, green, orange or yellow, for body and wings)

1 ball white

Small amount black

Small amount yellow (or orange for beak, if making yellow owl body)

Note: *Photographed models made with Aunt Lydia's® Crochet Thread Fashion 3™ in #175 Warm Blue, #775 Warm Rose, #625 Sage, #325 Tangerine, #423 Maize, #201 White and #12 Black.*

Size G/6 (4 mm) crochet hook (or size required for gauge)

Size D/3 (3.25 mm) crochet hook (or size required for gauge)

¾" (1.91 cm) bone or plastic ring

Tapestry needle

GAUGE

With larger hook and 2 strands of thread, 18 sc and 20 rows = 4" (10.16 cm)

STITCH GUIDE

Single crochet decrease (sc dec): [Insert hook in next st and draw up a lp] twice, YO and draw through all 3 lps on hook: sc dec made.

INSTRUCTIONS

Body (make 2: 1 for front and 1 for back)

Row 1 (right side): With larger hook and 1 strand each of desired color and white, ch 16, sc in back bump of 2nd ch from hook and in back bump of each rem ch across: 15 sc; ch 1, turn.

Row 2: Work 2 sc in first sc, sc in each sc across to last sc, 2 sc in last sc: 17 sc; ch 1, turn.

Row 3: Repeat Row 2: 19 sc.

Row 4: Repeat Row 2: 21 sc.

Row 5: Sc in each sc across; ch 1, turn.

Row 6: Repeat Row 2: 23 sc.

Rows 7 and 8: Repeat Row 5 twice.

Row 9: Repeat Row 2: 25 sc.

Rows 10 through 23: Repeat Row 5, 14 times.

Row 24: Sc dec in first 2 sc, sc in each sc across to last 2 sc, sc dec in last 2 sc: 23 sc; ch 1, turn.

Rows 25 through 28: Repeat Row 5, 4 times.

Rows 29 through 33: Repeat Rows 24 through 28: 21 sc.

Rows 34 through 38: Repeat Rows 24 through 28: 19 sc.

First Ear

Row 1 (right side): Sc dec in first 2 sc, sc in next 3 sc: 4 sc; ch 1, turn, leaving rem sts unworked.

Row 2: Sc dec in first 2 sc, sc in next 2 sc: 3 sc; ch 1, turn.

Row 3: Sc dec in first 2 sc, sc in next sc: 2 sc; ch 1, turn.

Row 4: Sc dec in 2 sc: 1 sc. Finish off; weave in ends.

Second Ear

Row 1 (right side): With right side facing and larger hook, skip next 9 sc on Row 38, join 1 strand each of desired color and white with sc in next sc, sc in next 2 sc, sc dec in last 2 sc: 4 sc; ch 1, turn.

Row 2: Sc in first 2 sc, sc dec in last 2 sc: 3 sc; ch 1, turn.

Row 3: Sc in first sc, sc dec in last 2 sc: 3 sc; ch 1, turn.

Row 4: Sc dec in 2 sc: 1 sc; ch 1, turn. Do not finish off.

Edging

Sc evenly around entire piece, increasing at top of ears and decreasing at inner corner of ears; join with sl st in first sc. Finish off; weave in ends.

Wings (make 2)

Row 1: With larger hook and 2 strands of desired color, ch 2, 2 sc in 2nd ch from hook: 2 sc; ch 1, turn.

Row 2: Sc in first sc, 2 sc in next sc: 3 sc; ch 1, turn.

Row 3: Work 2 sc in first sc, sc in each rem sc across: 4 sc; ch 1, turn.

Row 4: Sc in each sc across to last sc, 2 sc in last sc: 5 sc; ch 1, turn.

Rows 5 and 6: Repeat Rows 3 and 4: 6 sc in Row 5 and 7 sc in Row 6.

Row 7: Repeat Row 3: 8 sc.

Rows 8 through 14: Sc in each sc across; ch 1, turn.

Row 15: Sc dec in first 2 sc, sc in each rem sc across: 7 sc; ch 1, turn.

Row 16: Sc in each sc across to last 2 sc, sc dec in last 2 sc: 6 sc; ch 1, turn.

Rows 17 and 18: Repeat Rows 15 and 16: 5 sc in Row 17 and 4 sc in Row 18.

Row 19: Repeat Row 15: 3 sc.

Row 20: Sc in first sc, sc dec in last 2 sc: 2 sc; ch 1, turn.

Row 21: Sc dec in 2 sc: 1 sc; ch 1, turn on first wing. Do not turn on second wing.

Edging

Sc around entire piece, increasing at top and bottom corners; join with sl st in first sc. Finish off, leaving a long tail for sewing.

Eyes (make 2)

Round 1 (right side): With smaller hook and 1 strand of black, ch 2, 6 sc in 2nd ch from hook; join with sl st in first sc: 6 sc.

Round 2: Ch 1, 2 sc in each sc around; join as before: 12 sc.

Round 3: Ch 1, sc in first sc, 2 sc in next sc, [sc in next sc, 2 sc in next sc] 5 times; do not join: 18 sc.

Round 4: Sl st in each sc around; join with sl st in first sl st: 18 sl sts. Finish off; weave in ends.

Round 5: With right side facing, join 1 strand of white with sc in any sc on Round 3, working in sc on Round 3, sc in next sc, 2 sc in next sc, [sc in next 2 sc, 2 sc in next sc] 5 times; join with sl st in first sc: 24 sc.

Round 6: Ch 1, 2 sc in first sc, sc in next 3 sc, [2 sc in next sc, sc in next 3 sc] 5 times; do not join: 30 sc.

Round 7: Repeat Round 4: 30 sl sts. Finish off; weave in ends.

Round 8: With right side facing, join 1 strand of desired color with sc in any sc on Round 6, working in sc on Round 6, sc in next 3 sc, 2 sc in next sc, [sc in next 4 sc, 2 sc in next sc] 5 times; do not join: 36 sc.

Round 9: Repeat Round 4: 36 sl sts. Finish off, leaving a long tail for sewing.

Beak (make 1)

Row 1 (wrong side): With smaller hook and 1 strand of yellow (or orange for yellow owl body), ch 2, 2 sc in 2nd ch from hook: 2 sc; ch 1, turn.

Row 2: Sc in first sc, 2 sc in last sc: 3 sc; ch 1, turn.

Row 3: Sc in each sc across to last sc, 2 sc in first sc: 4 sc; ch 1, turn.

Row 4: Repeat Row 3: 5 sc.

Row 5: Sc in each sc across; ch 1, turn.

Row 6: Sc in each sc across to last 2 sc, sc dec in last 2 sc: 4 sc; ch 1, turn.

Rows 7 and 8: Repeat Row 6, 2 times: 3 sc in Row 7 and 2 sc in Row 8.

Row 9: Sc dec in 2 sc: 1 sc; ch 1, turn.

Edging

Sc around entire piece, increasing at top, bottom and center sides; join with sl st in first sc. Finish off, leaving a long tail for sewing.

Hanging Loop

With smaller hook and 1 strand of desired color, join with sc around bone ring, work 23 more sc around ring: 24 sc; join with sl st in first sc. Finish off, leaving a long tail for sewing.

Assembly

Referring to photo, center and sew beak in place between Rows 26 and 33 on body. Sew eyes in place, slightly overlapping top of beak. Pin wings to edge of front body piece between Rows 5 and 27 of body, with less curved edge of wings at edge of body. With wrong sides of front and back body pieces together, using larger hook and 2 strands of desired color, join with sc in center sc between ears, working through both layers of body and through outer edge of wings, as needed, sc evenly around entire body pieces, including ears, increasing at top of ears; join with sl st in first sc. Finish off; weave in ends. Using thread tail on wings, sew inner edge of wings to front of body. Center covered bone ring at top of body between ears and sew to top edge.

Dandy Dishcloth

Designed by Susan Lowman

The dishes will seem to get cleaner faster when washed with this dishcloth.

SKILL LEVEL

Easy

FINISHED SIZE

Approx 9½" (24.13 cm) square

MATERIALS

Size 3 crochet thread

[100% mercerized cotton, 150 yards (137.16 meters) per ball]

> 1 ball blue
>
> 1 ball white

Note: *Photographed model made with Aunt Lydia's® Crochet Thread Fashion 3™ #175 Warm Blue and #201 White*

Size I/9 (5.5 mm) crochet hook (or size required for gauge)

Tapestry needle

GAUGE

In FPdc, BPdc pattern, 15 sts and 10 rows = 4" (10.16 cm)

STITCH GUIDE

Front Post double crochet (FPdc): YO, insert hook from front to back to front around post of designated stitch and draw up a lp, (YO and draw through 2 lps on hook) twice: FPdc made.

Back Post double crochet (BPdc): YO, insert hook from back to front to back around post of designated stitch and draw up a lp, (YO and draw through 2 lps on hook) twice: BPdc made.

INSTRUCTIONS

Row 1 (right side): With 1 strand each of blue and white, ch 36, hdc in 3rd ch from hook (2 skipped chs count as first hdc), hdc in each rem ch across: 35 hdc; ch 2 (counts as hdc on following row here and throughout), turn.

Row 2: Skip first st, FPdc around next st, (BPdc around next st, FPdc around next st) 16 times, hdc in ch-sp: 17 FPdc, 16 BPdc and 2 hdc; ch 2, turn.

Rows 3 through 21: Repeat Row 2, 19 times. Do NOT ch 2 or turn at end of last row.

Edging

Ch 1, working along left edge, sc around post of last hdc on Row 21, ch 1, (sc in ch-sp on next row, ch 1, sc around post of hdc on next row, ch 1) 10 times; working in free lp of chs along bottom edge, sc in ch at base of same hdc, ch 1, (skip next ch, sc in next ch, ch 1) 17 times; working along right edge, sc in ch-sp on Row 1, ch 1, (sc around post of hdc on next row, ch 1, sc in ch-sp on next row, ch 1) 10 times; working along top edge, sc in 2nd ch of beg ch-2 on Row 21, ch 1, (skip next st, sc in next st, ch 1) 17 times; join with sl st in first sc: 78 sc and 78 ch-1 sps. Finish off; weave in ends.

Green Dishcloth

Designed by Treva G. McCain for Red Heart®

*It's not just the color that gives this dishcloth its name and meaning;
a dishcloth helps the environment.*

SKILL LEVEL

Easy ◼◼☐☐

FINISHED SIZE

Approx 8" x 8" (20.32 cm x 20.32 cm)

MATERIALS

Worsted weight cotton yarn (4)

[100% combed cotton, 2 ounces, 98 yards
(56.79 grams, 89.6 meters) per ball]

    1 ball multi green

Note: *Photographed model made with Red Heart®
Crème de la Crème® #965 Greentones*

Size I/9 (5.5 mm) crochet hook (or size required for gauge)

Yarn needle

GAUGE

16 sts = 4" (10.16 cm)

INSTRUCTIONS

Ch 32.

Row 1: Sc in 2nd ch from hook, * ch 1, skip next ch, sc in next ch; repeat from * across: 31 sts.

Row 2: Ch 1, turn, skip first sc, * sc in ch-1 space, ch 1, skip next sc; repeat from * across, end sc in beginning ch-1.

Rows 3 through 29: Repeat Row 2.

Row 30 (edging) : Ch 1, turn, 3 sc in first sc, sc in each st across to last st, 3 sc in last st, turn to work along side edge, sc 29 sts evenly spaced along side edge, turn to work along opposite edge of beg ch,
3 sc in first st of beg ch, sc in each st across last st, 3 sc in last st, turn to work along side edge, sc 29 sts evenly spaced along side edge, sl st to first st to join: 128 sc.

Finish off.

Starfish Dishcloth

Designed by Mary Ann Frits for Red Heart®

Almost too beautiful to use to clean the dirty dishes, it will, however, do the job.

SKILL LEVEL

Easy

FINISHED SIZE

Approx 9" (22.86 cm) in diameter

MATERIALS

Worsted weight cotton yarn

[100% combed cotton, 2.5 ounces, 125 yards (70.9 grams, 114.3 meters)per skein]

Note: *Photographed model made with Red Heart® Crème de La Crème™ #149 White(A), #500 Aqua (B) and #307 Tan (C)*

Size H/8 (5 mm) crochet hook (or size required for gauge)

Yarn needle

Stitch markers

GAUGE

17 sts = 4" (10.16 cm) in stitch pattern

INSTRUCTIONS

With A, ch 5, sl st in first ch to form a ring.

Round 1: * (Ch 9, sc in 2nd ch from hook, hdc in next ch, dc in next 6 chs) to make a point, sc in ring; repeat from * 4 times more: 5 points.

Finish off A. Place marker for beginning of round.

Round 2: Join B in 4th dc of previous point, ch 2 (counts as first dc), (YO, insert hook in next st, YO and draw lp through, YO, draw through 2 lps on hook) twice; YO, insert hook in ring, YO and draw lp through, YO, draw through 2 lps on hook; (YO, insert hook in next st, YO and draw lp through, YO, draw through 2 lps on hook) twice; YO and draw through all lps on hook, dc in next 4 sts in opposite edge of ch-9, skip last st, (3 dc, ch 3, 3 dc) in tip of point, skip next st, dc in next 4 sts; repeat from * 3 times more, (YO, insert hook in next st, YO and pull up lp, YO, draw through 2 lps) 5 times, YO and draw through all lps on hook), dc in next 4 sts, skip last st, (3 dc, ch 3, 3 dc) in tip of point, skip next st, dc in next 3 sts.

Round 3: Working in back lps only, * (YO, insert hook in next st, YO and draw lp through, YO, draw through 2 lps on hook) 3 times, YO and draw through all lps on hook; dc in next 5 sts, skip next st, (3 dc, ch 3, 3 dc) in next ch-3 sp, skip next st, dc in next 5 sts; repeat from * 4 times more.

Round 4: * (YO, insert hook in next st, YO, draw lp through, YO, draw through 2 lps on hook) 2 times, YO and draw through all lps on hook, dc in next 7 sts, skip next st, (3 dc, ch 3, 3 dc) in next ch-3 sp, dc in next 7 sts; repeat from * 4 times more. Finish off.

Edging

Round 1: Join C with sc in any ch-3 sp, 2 sc in same sp, * sc in next 9 sts, [YO, insert hook in next st, YO, draw lp through] 3 times, YO and draw through all lps on hook, sc in next 9 sts, 3 sc in next ch-3 sp; repeat from * 3 times more, sc in next 9 sts, (YO, insert hook in next st, YO, draw lp through) 3 times, YO and draw through all lps on hook, sc in next 9 sts, join with sl st in first sc.

Round 2: Ch 1, work reverse sc in each st around, join with sl st in first st. Finish off.

Finishing

Weave in ends.

Full of Color Dishcloth

This bright and cheerful dishcloth will help make any difficult task an easy one.

SKILL LEVEL

Easy

FINISHED SIZE

Approx 8½" x 9½" (21.59 cm x 24.13 cm)

MATERIALS

Worsted weight cotton yarn

[100% combed cotton, 2.5 ounces, 126 yards (71 grams, 115 meters) per ball]

    1 ball orange (A)

    1 ball yellow (B)

[100% combed cotton, 2 ounces, 99 yards (56.79 grams, 89.6 meters) per ball]

    1 ball multi (C)

Note: *Photographed model made with Red Heart® Crème de la Crème® #252 Brite Orange (A), #205 Golden Yellow (B) and #932 Popsicle Bright (C)*

Size I/9 (5.5 mm) crochet hook (or size required for gauge)

Yarn needle

GAUGE

4 dc = 1" (2.54 cm)

INSTRUCTIONS

Note: *When changing colors at the end of a row, work last stitch until 2 lps remain on hook; draw new color through. Cut old color.*

With Color A, ch 32.

Row 1 (right side): Sc in 2nd ch from hook and in each rem ch: 31 sc. Ch 2 (counts as first dc on following rows), turn.

Row 2: Dc in each sc. Ch 5 (counts as first dc and ch-3 sp on following rows), turn.

Row 3: Skip next 2 dc, sl st in next dc; * ch 5, skip next 2 dc, sl st in next dc; repeat from * 7 times more; ch 3, skip next 2 dc, dc in 2nd ch of turning ch-2. Ch 5, turn.

Row 4: Sl st in next ch-3 sp, ch 3; * sl st in next ch-5 sp, ch 3; repeat from * 8 times more, dc in 2nd ch of turning ch-5. Ch 2, turn.

Row 5: Dc in next ch-3 sp, 3 dc in each of next 9 ch-3 sps; dc in next ch-3 sp and in 2nd ch of turning ch-5, changing to Color B in last dc: 31 dc. Ch 1, turn.

Row 6: Sc in each dc and in 2nd ch of turning ch-2, changing to Color C in last sc. Ch 2, turn.

Row 7: Dc in each sc. Ch 2 (counts as an hdc on following row), turn.

Rows 8 through 12: Hdc in each dc, ch 2 (count as a dc on following rows); turn.

Row 13: Dc in each hdc and in 2nd ch of turning ch-2, changing to Color B in last dc. Ch 1, turn.

Row 14: Sc in each dc and in 2nd ch of turning ch-2, changing to Color A in last sc. Ch 2, turn.

Rows 15 through 18: Repeat Rows 2 through 5. At end of Row 18, do not change color.

Row 19: Sc in each dc and in 2nd ch of turning ch-2.

Finish off and weave in all ends.

Edging

Hold dishcloth with right side facing you and beg ch at top; join Color B in first unused lp of beg ch; ch 1, 3 sc in same chain as joining; working in unused lps of beg ch, sc in next 29 lps, 3 sc in next lp; † working across next side in each edge st and in sps formed by turning chs, skip next sc row, 2 sc in each of next 4 rows; sc in next row, 2 sc in next row; sc in next 5 rows, 2 sc in next row; sc in next row, 2 sc in each of next 4 rows, skip next sc row †; working across next side, 3 sc in next sc; sc in next 29 sc, 3 sc in next sc; repeat from † to † once; join in first sc.

Finish off and weave in ends.

Delightful Dishcloth

Designed by Treva G. McCain for Red Heart®

Who wouldn't want to do the dishes with this beautiful dishcloth?

SKILL LEVEL

Easy

FINISHED SIZE

Approx 9½" x 9½" (24.13 cm x 24.13 cm)

MATERIALS

Worsted weight cotton yarn

[100% combed cotton, 2.5 ounces, 126 yards (71 grams, 115 meters) per ball]

    1 ball red (A)

    1 ball green (B)

[100% combed cotton, 2 ounces, 99 yards (56.79 grams, 89.6 meters) per ball]

    1 ball multi red (C)

Note: *Photographed model made with Red Heart® Crème de la Crème®#905 Rally Red (A), #679 Spruce (B) and #992 Bowl of Cherries (C)*

Size I/9 (5.5 mm) crochet hook (or size required for gauge)

Yarn needle

GAUGE

16 sts = 4" (10.16 cm)

STITCH GUIDE

3-dc cluster: (YO, pull up a loop, pull through 2 loops) 3 times, YO, pull through all 4 loops on hook.

INSTRUCTIONS

With A, ch 32.

Row 1: Sc in 2nd ch from hook, * ch 1, skip next ch, sc in next ch; repeat from * across: 31 sts. Ch 1, turn.

Row 2: Skip first sc, *sc in ch-1 space, ch 1, skip next sc; repeat from *, end sc in beginning ch-1.

Rows 3 through 29: Repeat Row 2.

Row 30: 3 sc in first sc, sc in each st across to last st, 3 sc in last st, turn to work along side edge, sc 29 sts evenly spaced along side edge, turn to work along opposite edge of beg ch, 3 sc in first st of beg ch, sc in each st across to last st, 3 sc in last st, turn to work along side edge, sc 29 sts evenly spaced along side edge, sl st to first st to join: 128 sc. Finish off.

Row 31: With right side facing, join B in center st in any corner, ch 1, 3 sc in same st, *sc in each sc across to next corner sc, 3 sc in center sc of corner; repeat from * around, sl st in first sc to join: 136 sc. Finish off.

Row 32: With right side facing, join C in center st in any corner, * [skip next sc, 3-dc cluster in next sc, ch 1] across to last sc before center sc of corner, skip last sc, ([3-dc cluster, ch 2] 3 times) in center sc of corner; repeat from * around, sl st in first st to join. Finish off.

Row 33: With right side facing, join B in any ch-space, ch 1, sc in same space, ch 2, (sc in next ch-space, ch 2) around, sl st to first st to join. Finish off.

Weave in ends.

Dishcloth in the Round

Designed by Susan Lowman

Working around and around, the bowls do get clean.

SKILL LEVEL

Easy

FINISHED SIZE

Approx 10" (25.40 cm) diameter

MATERIALS

Size 3 crochet thread

[100% mercerized cotton, 150 yards (137.16 meters) per ball]

    1 ball pink

    1 ball white

Note: *Photographed model made with Aunt Lydia's® Crochet Thread Fashion 3™ #775 Warm Rose and #201 White.*

Size I/9 (5.5 mm) crochet hook (or size required for gauge)

Tapestry needle

GAUGE

Rounds 1 through 4 = 4½" (11.43 cm) diameter

STITCH GUIDE

Front Post double crochet (FPdc): YO, insert hook from front to back to front around post of designated stitch and draw up a lp, [YO and draw through 2 lps on hook] twice: FPdc made.

Back Post double crochet (BPdc): YO, insert hook from back to front to back around post of designated stitch and draw up a lp, [YO and draw through 2 lps on hook] twice: BPdc made.

INSTRUCTIONS

Round 1 (right side): With 1 strand each of pink and white, ch 4, 11 dc in 4th ch from hook (3 skipped chs count as first dc); join with sl st in 4th ch of beg ch-4: 12 dc.

Round 2: Ch 4 (counts as dc and ch-1 sp), FPdc around next st, ch 1, [BPdc around next st, ch 1, FPdc around next st, ch 1] 5 times; join with sl st in 3rd ch of beg ch-4: 6 FPdc, 5 BPdc, 1 dc and 12 ch-1 sps.

Round 3: Sl st in next ch-1 sp, ch 3 (counts as hdc and ch-1 sp); * BPdc around next st, ch 1, hdc in next ch-1 sp, ch 1, FPdc around next st, ch 1**, hdc in next ch-1 sp, ch 1; repeat from * around, ending last repeat at **; join with sl st in 2nd ch of beg ch-3: 6 FPdc, 6 BPdc, 12 hdc and 24 ch-1 sps.

Round 4: Ch 2 (counts as hdc), hdc in same ch as joining, ch 1; * FPdc around next st, ch 1, 2 hdc in next st, ch 1, BPdc around next st, ch 1**, 2 hdc in next st, ch 1; repeat from * around, ending last repeat at **; join with sl st in 2nd ch of beg ch-2: 6 FPdc, 6 BPdc, 24 hdc and 24 ch-1 sps.

Round 5: Ch 3 (counts as hdc and ch-1 sp here and throughout), FPdc around next st, ch 1; * BPdc around next st, ch 1, FPdc around next st, ch 1; repeat from * around; join with sl st in 2nd ch of beg ch-3: 18 FPdc, 17 BPdc, 1 hdc and 36 ch-1 sps.

Round 6: Ch 3, BPdc around next st, ch 1; * FPdc around next st, ch 1, BPdc around next st, ch 1; repeat from * around; join as before: 17 FPdc, 18 BPdc, 1 hdc and 36 ch-1 sps.

Round 7: Ch 3; * hdc in next ch-1 sp, ch 1, FPdc around next st, ch 1 **, BPdc around next st, ch 1; repeat from * around, ending last repeat at **; join: 18 FPdc, 17 BPdc, 19 hdc and 54 ch-1 sps.

Round 8: Ch 3, FPdc around next st, ch 1, BPdc around next st, ch 1; * (FPdc around next st, ch 1) twice, BPdc around next st, ch 1; rep from * around; join: 35 FPdc, 18 BPdc, 1 hdc and 54 ch-1 sps.

Round 9: Ch 3, BPdc around next st, ch 1, FPdc around next st, ch 1; * (BPdc around next st, ch 1) twice, FPdc around next st, ch 1; rep from * around; join: 18 FPdc, 35 BPdc, 1 hdc and 54 ch-1 sps.

Round 10: Repeat Round 8.

Round 11: (Sl st, ch 1, sc) in next ch-1 sp, ch 2; * sc in next ch-1 sp, ch 2; rep from * around; join with sl st in first sc: 54 sc and 54 ch-2 sps. Finish off; weave in ends.